Re-Membering

"In the midst of life we are in death."
Book of Common Prayer, 1662, Burial of the Dead

poems by

Alice A. Hildebrand

Finishing Line Press
Georgetown, Kentucky

Re-Membering

"In the midst of life we are in death."
Book of Common Prayer, 1662, Burial of the Dead

Copyright © 2022 by Alice A. Hildebrand
ISBN 978-1-64662-707-3 First Edition
All rights reserved under International and Pan-American Copyright Conventions. No part of this book may be reproduced in any manner whatsoever without written permission from the publisher, except in the case of brief quotations embodied in critical articles and reviews.

ACKNOWLEDGMENTS

Thank you to my parents, Edith and Ernest Hildebrand, for encouraging my writing; to my son James Hildebrand for enduring my grumpiness when he was small and I was working on a piece; to my friend Mary Dillon for always believing in me; and to my husband Allen Myers for his support in so many ways. Thanks also to Nancy Avery Dafoe for gently nudging me into the modern world of publishing. And many thanks to the staff of Finishing Line Press, especially Leah Maines, Kevin Maines and Christen Kincaid, for making the process of publication smooth and unintimidating.

Pg. 14: Russell, George William. "The Great Breath", *Collected Poems by A.E.* London, Macmillan, 1913.

Publisher: Leah Huete de Maines
Editor: Christen Kincaid
Cover Art: Alice A. Hildebrand
Author Photo: Allen C. Myers
Cover Design: Elizabeth Maines McCleavy

Order online: www.finishinglinepress.com
also available on amazon.com

Author inquiries and mail orders:
Finishing Line Press
PO Box 1626
Georgetown, Kentucky 40324
USA

Table of Contents

Crows 1

The Island 2

The Necklace 5

Autumn 6

Undoing 7

Within Your Body 8

Trip to Tinkers, Sunset, August 11

Litany for My Mother's Death 13

Remembered You 22

Crows

The clink of glass draws me
to the kitchen. You
are wrapping empties in newspaper
and bundling them into a box.
I did not mean to catch you
at this; silently, we feel
for safer footing. You move
to shield your booty;
I play dumb.

At the house where you raised me
a blue spruce stood
at the edge of the yard.
Your clothesline ended there.
From my window in whichever
cold, wet season, spring or autumn,
I could see the tree hung
with crows and threads of icy mist.
Harsh, raucous, they flapped
from bough to sodden yellow grass.

You stand in that window with me,
for a moment, signifying something
clearly—your own secret,
then and now, just what that something is.

You strode through my childhood
I scurried before you, a wind-tossed leaf.
Crow-like, you perched above me, dark,
convinced, commenting. Years later,
I understand your abbreviated flight—
from tree to ground, from ground
to tree—you believed
your voice to be unbeautiful,
so sang loudly instead.

The Island

The Island sits square on the horizon
spread from east to west, southern to every place else,
last outpost before Spain.
Seen behind all the other islands, the frivolous, small ones
and from this distance, silent,
its blue height could be thought to brood.
But it's just there. Long before I came along,
my great-uncle died at sea and after that
the family never had a boat, not even one for rowing
although neighbors were generous with theirs.
His sister, who owned the place then—
called in these parts "a camp," meaning small,
unfinished—never approved of boats.
It seemed there wasn't much she did approve of,
but on a summer that my father's two-week holiday
matched fair not foggy weather
we took a borrowed dory
out to where Western Mountain and Cadillac,
unforeshortened by anything, loom in the east
and rowed southward, rounding the rocks
off the bar to Green Island Light.
The bold shore of the Island slipped hazily into view.
I exhaled, not knowing until then
I'd held my breath. When I was old enough
to take the hurried low-tide walk over the bar alone,
one small island of stunted trees and gulls to the next
out to what seemed like the middle of the bay,
I never let myself
look at the southern sky until I knew
that it would be there.

Growing up I never really thought about him,
the man who'd made the model of the whaling ship
I was occasionally permitted to take down
from its place on the mantel

and sail across the linoleum "carpet" of the living room.
He'd drowned off the coast of Greenland on a September day,
sailing around the world in his own small boat with three friends.
I never considered that the woman we drove up here
for vacation with us every year was the older sister of that dead man.
My husband, coming late into the claustrophobia of my family
commented on our lack of boats.
It would have been inconceivable—my always-broke parents,
Dad so overwhelmed by mechanical things—
we weren't the sort of people who could own boats.
My youthful tousled father in his Marine Corps fatigues
gamely worked at re-puttying the windows;
great-aunt fussed that he should just relax.
My parents, who through the winters seemed only to love books,
each year fought the entropy of an old building by the sea,
my father on a ladder, my mother
in the thicket of what had been the lawn
happier with the alder shears
than trying to talk with the great-aunt
and I with my sneakers always wet,
watching them all, dreaming of how I would make my escape;
not from them, but from everything
everything land-bound.

Not until I was sixteen or so did we ever go out
to see the Island for ourselves, and then only
because some visiting artistic friends
unlikely people for my family to know
invited us. The great-aunt gone by then, there was no one to say,
"We've come all this way from Hartford and New York;
why not stay put?" As the mailboat neared the landing,
the Island too big, but seen up close, with common buildings—
homes, fish houses, a wharf with derricks—too small,
I lit a cigarette. Ashore, my mother wanted no part
of renting a bicycle from the General Store.

"Well, it's five miles to the other end," the proprietress said.
Leaving the others, the formidable painterly wife
strapping lunch onto the dented fender of a well-used Schwinn,
my mother set out down the dirt road.
"Come on," she said to me. "Let's hitch;"
a dozen or so cars in the whole place.
An old Chrysler appeared, we got in.
For her sake, the Island could be ordinary
the first time that I was ever there.

The Necklace

In the yellow room the dark furniture shone
with the life of loved wood.
My mother stood on Sunday mornings
before the oval mirror fogged from within by age
and designed for shorter people.
She bent her knees, leaned back
and tucked her chin, in order to see her face.
I sat at the foot of the bed
my Mary Janes dangling, socks already
slipping down and wished
one day to have long, silky, nylon-covered legs
and hipbones poking out like that.

She looked severely at herself held
in the misty glass and patted
her short hair briskly. Liquids and powders
created new skin, new fragrance
and above the rouge, her blue eyes danced
as she pinned on and fastened
her few pieces of "good" jewelry.

Last week she gave me
a necklace, it must have belonged
to someone on Daddy's side—
cut glass, strung on a tiny silver chain
narrow rings of brass between the crystal beads.
I've worn it twice and already
the tarnish has rubbed off the brass;
the beads lie in the hollow
of my collarbones just as
they lay in hers, just as
I remember this necklace
made with a craft forgotten now,
each bead cut with twelve facets top and bottom,
a tiny carved flower on the clasp.

Autumn

Sunday, a drive on which
both my parents
point out the brilliant yellow drape, bittersweet
engulfing somber spruce while we
don't talk about what the doctor said on Friday—
then Monday, my son
upon a dusk-dulled soccer field
his hair a plume of gold and silver light—
and Tuesday, a yearling bear, black,
round-eared, on all fours
against scarlet sumac—

all this, all this and I
am tired of blooming, after a long summer.
The geraniums, still fiery red
put out smaller, then smaller flowers.
October lies down on the pale bleached grass.

I await November's sullen sky
bare twigs and branches, brown leaves.
Squirrels seeking shelter
will dangle from the water-beaded naked curves
of the maple trees. I wait.

Undoing

And through all this
undoing of my mother's life,
it becomes autumn—7:15 AM now when the sun
cracks through the tall green trees
to light the blowsy overblown garden;
been in the forties two nights in a row
and the last few nights, I've heard coyotes
under the huge pink moon.

I wash the dishes at my parents' house,
realizing these things all alone, she always sleeping
he upstairs at his books, or off doing errands;
remembering how many times
my mother called us three together
to look at light—
the sky at dawn, or just after sunset
flamingo, rose, peach, violet
each time as though it were the first.

Perhaps the last? She's asleep in her final bed
these many weeks now, and will there be more to come?
Autumn unpins itself
throughout the starry sky
a rustle of leaves gone
on the wind, a confusion
of temperatures, airs, light;
9:22 AM this day was the mid-point, they say;
heading out of the easy side
down the hill into winter's grip.

Within Your Body

I once grew within your body
a perfect home;
food, air, water came to me
through the offices of your blood.
What did I see inside your womb
through then unopened eyelids
absolute darkness or walls like earlobes,
like finger webbings;
like the light through a horn window,
or windows of thinly sliced stone?
A noisy place, the rush of this
fluid, the emptying of that chamber, the pulse, the beat
of the heart... perhaps within the earth it's like that, too
worms tunneling, beetles scratching, water pooling
then drying up, dirt contracting, the whole settling
in upon itself, then rising; pelted by rain, shot through
with ice crystals, cracked and made separate by sun.

We only go there when we're in the grave,
without eyes, without ears, no nerve endings,
no sense organs, no animal part left
with which to know, and yet somehow
we call it "back to the earth", as though
we once had lived inside it, as though
that liquid, airless place we do begin in,
98.6 and so mammalian, was just gardening,
a matter of pressure and warmth, like seeds
that sprout alone.

Animal mother, to your body I once clung
seeking the nipple, undirected hands
scrabbling against soft flesh
or, older: directed hands patting
the beloved breast, lips letting go
to seek your face and smile; and then,

the sinews of your neck in which I buried my face
to cry and be comforted
your knee on which I leaned
your brisk hands arranging me;
a kiss good bye. The advent of language
years in which the physical
was just a pat, a hug until
your dying time.

I was immersed in you again, your body;
your body, about which you were always so frank
a nurse's frankness, why bother with subterfuge
frank about bodies in general.
At first we talked
you sat in a chair, clipped to oxygen
I passed you things
from a cardboard box;
we told stories, even wondered
together about death.
I watched each breath, each function
as it happened on time, late, then not at all
bathing, changing, turning you in bed,
you but not you, your eyes tight shut
holding your hand, stroking your arm
chanting, "I love you, I love you"
thinking, "You can go now," thinking
"But where are you going, will I be able
to find you again?"

When the nurse came, one last time,
to officially pronounce your death,
she offered to wash and dress your body,
said gently to me as we worked together,
"This isn't the first time you've done this."
My mother's body!

        that I handled carefully
        lovingly, but like a professional
        how could I not
        finish the job we'd begun
        every inch of the way
        blood, sweat, pee, tears
        mine, yours, you didn't weep
        over my diapers, I didn't weep
        over yours
And so, dressed in a clean nightgown,
you were placed in your coffin, my father and I
helped to settle you, a small pillow under your head
a blue and white shawl for cushioning.
My son and my husband
carried you out to the dawn
where the man from the crematorium
quietly waited, and the sky was red.

All these attentions to the animal nature,
its spent husk motionless in a dark wooden box
the once remembered velvet, then paper feeling
of your skin, the mother smells, that elastic
strength in hand and leg and arm. . .

you were dispersed, your body baked
and baked, all water gone, all softness, made absolutely
incorruptible, dispersed to sacred ash
into which I reached, curious, finding
no sense of you at all, just minerals.
We wove you into the ground, one small handful
at a time and now you're buried.
I can't see the earth as womb or home
but rather, I feel you in the sky;
maybe, although we begin in darkness,
we end in openness and light.

Trip to Tinkers, Sunset, August

At day's end this day, we fled
the ordinary summer world,
lawn mower, neighbor's voice, crow caw;
off to a place made silent
by constant wind
its work with water—a trip to Tinkers,
empty island spread along the edge
of our shore's outlook to the eastern sky.

*All through last January we sat
in a room made silent
by the sigh of the oxygen machine,
waiting, as my mother
made her way towards death;
her bed the altar,
the workplace of our contemplation.
In what had been the dining room,
the old mahogany pushed aside
made way for steel and plastic.
The walls still hung with voiceless ancestors
contained unvarying light;
a dim glow of sun through thick curtains
or her small lamp at night.
We worked with her, dumb as draft animals
right up to the edge
but she traveled over it alone.*

Three hours row in stiff chop out
and now, returning to the placid breadth of continent
over a flattening sea,
surrounded by the whole sky, I lean
against the uppermost bit
of the boat's high curved stern, hands in pockets
against August sunset chill, and watch my husband
dip the oars into cold dark water.

I watch the seeming green water
prove itself clear with each stroke of the oars,
watch the clouds bleed out to north and south
while the bulk of land a mile ahead of us grows black.
I sit beneath the opening sky

    feel it open wider and go on forever,
    over the evening land,
    earth so swift upon its axis,
    daylight peeling away westward,
    night surging up behind from the east.
I see the dulled face of the horizon
not yet animate with stars—
my mother's face, turned ashen when all motion ceased.
over my shoulder, the so familiar mountains
on the island in the east
turn inconsequential in the absence of the light

    to see the sky
    and know it not as ceiling but as throat; an opening
    freed by twilight from blue color spotted with white clouds,
    comforting as a nursery rhyme;
    to see that painted surface turn to vapor and disappear...

    to be swallowed by the darkness
    racing after
    and yet be unafraid...

An hour and a half past midnight
on the birthday she wished to reach
we sang and said good-bye once more
to her in whatever place she had been lingering,
without speech, without gesture, yet still
herself. Something passed
across her face, and emptiness grew deeper.
I leaned down and turned off the oxygen tank.

Litany for My Mother's Death

FIRST VOICE

See the sunset sky, it looks solid;
clouds unbelievably furled and scattered
creating coral colored columns and canyons,
providing rose mist to float amongst them
a mirage of desert landscape in mid air.

Beneath, the stark spruce and maple
edging mown fields already white with dew
allow pale yellow openings of brilliance
in the black embroidery of their branches.

See how each house
is uncommon and perfect
set apart by a ragged tangle of wildflowers,
or chubby antique kettles of marigold and fern;
the torn tarpaper and the split window frame,
the porch glider or the three new cars;
all equally beloved and glowing
works of art
made by innocent hands.

Oh see, in this warm re-creating Light
which touches all lovingly and without favor
as God's eyes do touch us,
how we are made, and made over newly.
Oh see, and find yourself again
in childhood twilights:
stopping at play
between the houses
watching the benevolence of sun
depart in splendor
to bring the quiet night.

There, where childhood sleeps
between the wings and feathers
of the mother birds,
the screen door bangs closed
on summer darkness.
Inside that lighted house awaits the ritual of bath
and bedtime slides between white cotton sheets.

Monday, August, 1929—Journal of Edith Mae Hettema, 18 years old

> *I am quite tired tonight. I feel rather lonesome but before going to bed I want to record here two lines which are poignantly beautiful and express ideally the way day ends here at the lake.*
>
> *"Its edges foamed with amethyst and rose*
> *Withers once more the old blue flower of day"*   A.E.
>
> *The sunsets I have witnessed this summer have been symphonies of color and the lake is never so beautiful as when the mountains surrounding it are topped off by clouds of every hue.*
>
> *"The old blue flower of day" withers slowly leaving salmon-pink, shell-green and lavender banners aflame in the sky for hours. I love to drift slowly across the serene lake and keep my eyes fixed on the horizon until the first evening star appears.*

SECOND VOICE

> falling headlong, oh to be
> falling
> headlong into sleep—
> my lover
> now that again I sleep alone;
> tumbling

into that most thorough embrace
(although we *do* wish
eventually, to awaken,
not ready yet, perpetually
not ready
to be dead.)

sleep! all that white, smooth softness
waiting in my bed, those pillows
those sheets used just enough
to smell familiar and yet still be fresh;
the welter of blankets and comforters
quilts my mother made—
a weight of warmth
against cool darkness. . .

THIRD VOICE

When we were drugging you
against the panic of your lungs closing down
I learned to cradle you
each time we had to move you in the bed.
At first, it seemed that you fell upwards
from sleep daze into fear, poor thin arms grabbing
at the air, eyes opening. I held you
more closely than perhaps
you would once have wished—
by the time I came along,
you were not a snuggler—
my round arm against the angles of your shoulder blades
my cheek against yours.
I told you that I loved you then;
you never stirred. Twice,
a single tear ran down your cheek.

FIRST VOICE

In photographs of sleeping children
even the faces day cramps with rage
are slack and quiet in animal repose.
In sleep there is that silencing
of the voices whispering bleak counterpoint
to the song of days.

August 1929
I can dream such dreams as all youth does, but still I fill my days
with nursing training, spend my free time reading, talking, serving,
and doing all the things which are part of life in this age...
I spend time thinking of the peace program, Chinese Russian hostilities,
  the control of England by the Labor Party, the condition of Germany
  under her load of war debts, the enmities of France and Italy,
the Hoover policy, prohibition, aviation, the advances of science,
psychology, and all the events that are taking place in this year of 1929...
Being a part of this great program called life it is impossible
to stand apart and even get a fleeting glimpse of the whole ceremony.
Perhaps with the discernment and experience of maturity I will
comprehend God's pattern of life a little.

SECOND VOICE

The boy picks his way up the blue rime
of the frozen hill each morning
behind him the icy runnels are shot
with dawn. Once, after a storm,
he stopped at the curve
where the gradient lessens
and stood there between
top and bottom, looking up
through snow curved branches at parakeet-blue sky.

He did a little dance, there in between;
everything felt right-sized, he knew where
he belonged. I watched him, and I

saw his smallness, the flash of his red cap
I saw how he climbed, step by step, with the long road
unfurling, and the steep part yet to come.

FIRST VOICE

Whatever passions now crumple our faces
as we sit through lives
where job and beer and anger,
exhaustion, succeed each other
rubbing bare the fabric of the years
there is still that continuing moment
in which God affirms the covenant
and we re-gain our Childhood
without the ancient legacies
of hatred and of fear.

THIRD VOICE

>	Crow speech, naked trees, first light
>	sliver of moon in the morning sky;
>	wind from the west,
>	hush of the sea, pink cloud riding by.

I read your journals all that last week
by the narcissus in bloom on the kitchen table
by the bed holding your hot, still hand—
oh soul on God's journey
oh animal body
oh mother of mine

SECOND VOICE

At night my son surrenders willingly
to sheets printed with cats
and smoothed by me, pillows
turned cool side up, hot water bottle
tucked by toes. I make
this world of sleep for him each night;
a beady-eyed plush animal,
worn hairless, a blanket
that has absorbed breast milk, tears
sloughed-off skin, saliva, pee

THIRD VOICE

First we dressed you
in a peach colored night gown, then
we wrapped you
in your Delft blue and white blanket,
and lifted you into the new pine box,
golden and smelling slightly of varnish;
a good honest smell for a carpenter's daughter,
my husband said. Under your head
we put the small pillow
that you had held against your aching chest.

SECOND VOICE

A dreamer, I climb
the mountain of sleep, white sleep, blue
sleep, heavy sleep furred as if with snowflakes
weariness softening my limbs, soft sleep

I climb and sink through
the crust of this mountain crumbles
the cavern is hollow and I may fall

FIRST VOICE

God is my Father, my Mother, myself
I shall not want;

God is all of us, we are One
beside still waters;
at rest in green pastures.

The passage of the Light
restores our soul and leads us
in the paths of righteousness
for the sake of love.

And when we walk
in emptiness and confusion
we are comforted
by the ceaseless melody
that needs nothing of us.
The light and the air
rain down on all,
filling us beyond measure.

And surely there, in that House,
we shall be good, and merciful,
and dwell in peace forever.

SECOND VOICE

On my bed is the lavender quilt
my mother made. My cats, those expert sleepers,
spend whole days there, tiger bellies lavishly stretched
over the printed calico. Outside,
the sky gathers itself
for another snowstorm.
Tonight I will lie quietly
curled on my side alone,
but not sleeping a virginal sleep,
light, quick dissolving like white sugar—
no, mine is the sleep of the mother polar bear
in her breath cave of snow, mine
are the heavy paws that pat gently,
urge sleep.

December 1929
> *Before I begin the work that is waiting for me tonight*
> *I am going to write in this diary.*
> *I cannot become accustomed to the spectacle of death,*
> *it is so tragic and sorrowful. Last night a sweet little baby died and*
> *I experienced a feeling of helplessness and poignant grief.*
> *But such an experience causes reflection and I thought about love.*
> *Love conquers. . .*

November 1930
> *I find joy in my work. . .I have the firm conviction*
> *that life is good—the beauties of the natural world, the love of friends,*
> *the beneficence of sleep, the reward of work well-done, the acquisition*
> *of knowledge and the fellowship with the Infinite make living*
> *very worthwhile. . .*

And, I am learning to dance! And am really progressing!

THIRD VOICE

Mother, I saw you treading lightly
on a swath of winter sky,
barefoot, in a gown of vapor,
holding its train in your arms.
I saw your smile of great delight.

Remembered You

Three years ago today we remembered you
re-membered you, gave you flesh
who'd died, been all burned up
but a three pound box, ash and slivers of bone;
re-membered you, a hundred or so of us—
basket of flowers, spring bulbs that you loved
your favorite hymns—or at least, ones
that reminded us of you.
I wrote the eulogy, not trusting anyone
but myself to get it right, sat in my pew thinking
"Yes," not feeling much of anything
while my husband read the words I'd written.

Dead in February, remembered in May
buried that July
        turning trowel-fulls of dry summer earth
        dipping my hands into the clinging, gritty powder,
        putting you, as you had wished, directly into the earth,
        my bare knees scratched by stubbled grass
        under a sky bleached with heat—

the box your ashes had come home in
sat empty in the corner of my bedroom for three years.
We burned it this past winter
on the beach in front of the house
cardboard, it opened
in graceful black petals tipped with flame
disappeared featherlight, grey white
absorbed by the breeze:
unlike the weight of your long bones
unlike the heft of you, still, even reduced by fire.

Alice Aldrich Hildebrand grew up in Briarcliff Manor, New York, where she began to write poetry as a child. Her family always summered on the coast of Maine, and Hildebrand moved there permanently in 1978.

In 1969 Hildebrand received a National Council of Teachers of English Award for her poetry. At Kirkland College in Clinton, New York, she majored in Creative Writing and worked with artists-in-residence Denise Levertov, and Naomi Lazard. In 1973 she received the Watrous Award for poetry at Kirkland. After graduating in 1973, Hildebrand moved to New Mexico, where she worked as a seamstress for Levi Strauss. Two years later she moved to North Carolina and continued to work as a seamstress in the garment industry. In 1976 she received the North Carolina Poetry Association award.

Since moving to Maine, Hildebrand has worked on her fiction with Helen Yglesias, and participated in a poetry reading with Daniel Hoffman. Her stories and poetry have appeared in *Killick Stones*, a collection of Maine island writing; *Lost Orchard;* and *Puckerbrush Review*. In 1987 she won the Hampton's International Award for poetry. She graduated from Bangor Theological Seminary in 1987 with a Master of Divinity degree. In 1993 she was Recorded as a Minister in the Society of Friends (Quaker), and received Privilege of Call in the United Church of Christ in 2003. In addition to having served as pastor for three different churches, she is a Board Certified Chaplain who has worked in several hospitals, in home-based medical hospice and palliative care, and as a Pediatric Chaplain. In her capacity as chaplain, she has published research in the *Journal of Healthcare Chaplaincy* ("A Qualitative Study of Patient and Family Perceptions of Chaplain Presence During Post-Trauma Care"), and contributed a chapter to *Spiritual Care in Practice*.

She is married, and has three sons and four grandchildren.

www.ingramcontent.com/pod-product-compliance
Lightning Source LLC
LaVergne TN
LVHW041524070426
835507LV00012B/1797